I0475842

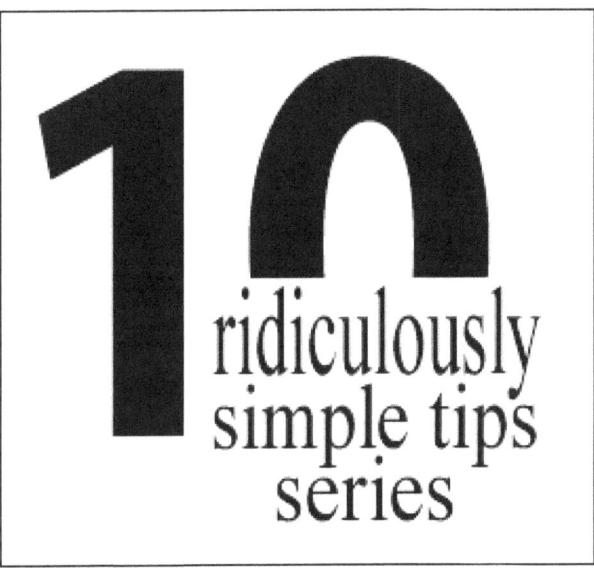

2

10 ridiculously simple tips

Business Plans

Straightforward Information in Condensed Format

★ ARTISTIC / BUSINESS SERIES ★
created by John DeGaetano

ARTISTIC / BUSINESS SERIES
created by John DeGaetano

About the Series

The "*ridiculously simple*" series is designed to give you straightforward information on a variety of subjects in a condensed format. These books help you be yourself, and guides your vision on the artistic/creative side of your personality as relates to a business setting. Most experts agree that art finds it's way into the hearts of many, however to make it as an entrepreneur and do whatever it is you truly love, the business side always comes into play… and vice versa. How you treat your business side of things is really the key to success.

About this Book

10 Ridiculously Simple Tips: Business Plans touches on all the things you need to know about writing a business plan, set goals for the business and ultimately build the business of your dreams, or help someone else write a successful plan. We'll give you 10 of the most important tips to consider when determining exactly what to plan for in content along with style/guideline considerations as it relates to the various types of businesses.

Putting the Pieces Together

Don't worry, you're not alone… putting the pieces together and writing a great business plan is intimidating for everyone.

What makes the task of writing a plan so difficult is deciding what to include, what not to, what to highlight, what to de-emphasize, etc. If you truly want to work in the field of your choice, then writing it… is a necessity. Next comes the investment and how you handle start up costs and frugal planning every step of the way. Being your everyday self yet displaying focused enthusiasm in strategy is the best approach. With a business plan, there is such thing as going overboard with far too many details. Format should be a living, breathing document – and changeable so that your business can survive in the marketplace.

What does Wikipedia say?

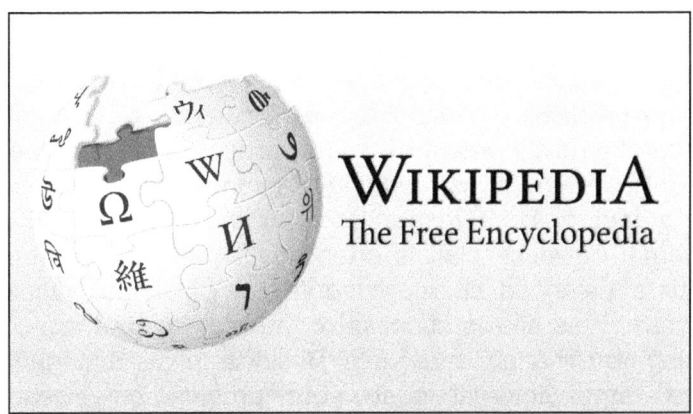

Business Plan

A Business Plan is a formal statement of business goals, reasons they are attainable, and plans for reaching them. It may also contain background information about the organization or team attempting to reach those goals.

Business plans may target changes in perception and branding by the customer, client, taxpayer, or larger community. When the existing business is to assume a major change or when planning a new venture, a 3 to 5 year business plan is required, since investors will look for their investment return in that timeframe.

Business plans may be internally or externally focused. Externally focused plans target goals that are important to external stakeholders, particularly financial stakeholders. They typically have detailed information about the organization or team attempting to reach the goals. With for-profit entities, external stakeholders include investors and customers. External stakeholders of non-profits include donors, or government agencies, taxpayers, government agencies, and/or other international lending bodies.

Internally focused business plans target intermediate goals required to reach the external goals. They may cover the development of a new product, a new service, a new IT system, a restructuring of finance, the refurbishing of a factory or a restructuring of the organization. An internal business plan is often developed in conjunction with a balanced scorecard or a list of critical success factors. This allows success of the plan to be measured using non-financial measures. Business plans that identify and target internal goals, but provide only general guidance on how they will be met are called strategic plans.

Operational plans describe the goals of an internal organization, working group or department. Project plans, sometimes known as project frameworks, describe the goals of a particular project. They may also address the project's place within the organization's larger strategic goals.

*Information above courtesy of Wikipedia, the free encyclopedia.

Interesting Facts

Writing a business plan and its value is often debated with entrepreneurs. Very successful businesses have been launched with a well-thought-out business plan, yet you can find equally successful ones that were launched in a garage somewhere with just a few raw notes.

However, statistics show that those who completed business plans were nearly twice as likely to successfully grow their businesses or obtain capital as those who didn't write a plan.

To be more specific, more than one third of them secured a loan or investment capital. And well over half of them have grown their business in the past five years. The numbers to success to businesses without a formal business plan amount to only half of those that do.

"Except in rare cases a small number of cases, all this research indicates that the type of entrepreneur who completes a business plan is also more likely to be a better entrepreneur and run a more successful business."

The popular reasons to start your own business;

- Personal achievement as their primary motivation for success or looking for financial stability.
- Got their idea from a previous job that inspired them.
- Interested at the same time in building skills in technology or other areas.
- Interested in the personal freedom of owning a business and potential growth associated with it.
- While others want to give back to their community and develop great business relationships.

So there you have it: you're better off and twice as likely to grow your business or achieve funding if you have taken the time to write a business plan.

<u>The Good News:</u> is... if you are willing to learn how to create an excellent business plan, with a little extra effort, you will usually get an even better response from prospective investors, financial institutions, community and customers alike.

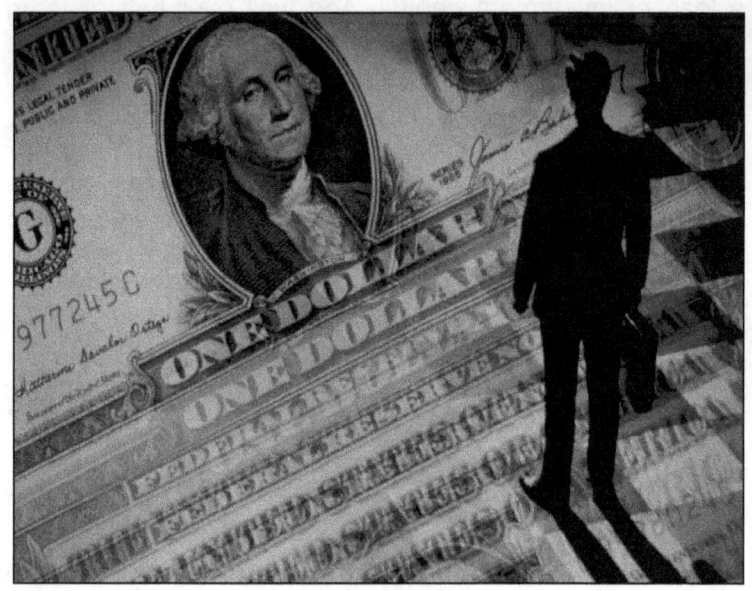

Statistics

General Business Statistics

As a business owner, you will need a solid understanding of your market and current economic conditions to plan for business growth and success. The SBA Dept at sba.gov has a wealth of information to help you indentify your market and demographic information. The following resources provide statistics on a variety of U.S. industries and business conditions (information courtesy of the SBA Dept.)

North American Industry Classification System (NAICS Codes) – Provides the standard used by Federal statistical agencies in classifying business establishments for the purpose of collecting, analyzing and publishing statistical data related to the U.S. business economy. Information includes definition of each industry and background material.

FedStats – Offers a full range of official statistical information produced by more than 100 agencies. Site provides data and trend information on topics such as economic and population trends, crime, education, health care, aviation safety, energy use, farm production and more.

Statistical Abstract of the United States – Presents an authoritative and comprehensive summary of statistics on the social, political and economic conditions in the United States.

Statistics of U.S. Businesses – Features a collection of data files created from U.S. Census County Business Patterns, an annual series that provides sub-national economic data by industry.

So why is a plan so important? Answer: Economic Impact. Based on their records, the U.S. Bureau of Labor and Statistics summarizes a business chief goal is to attract, motivate and retain the most qualified employees and match them to jobs for which they are best suited. This translates into dollars and cents… ultimately, Economic Impact through reputation and planning.

"A business plan reflects the potential success an investor can expect from the business."

Tips...

OK then, after your objectives are determined, prioritize the content of your business plan to suit those objectives. You have a small window of time to get the interest of an investor, landlord, banker, family member, etc so being detailed and extremely focused is essential. A lengthy business plan (over 40 pages) does not necessarily translate to higher potential of success; it may even encourage the reader to skim though or by pass the document just based on the sight of its length.

To successfully launch a truly great business plan, follow these 10 helpful tips:

Draft a Business Summary of Ideas and Overviews

Creating a business summary not for the plan itself but for your own guidelines can be tricky, especially in the planning stages. These are the planning stages of your concept, a potential business model, an overview of where your business might lead.

If you already own an existing business, summarizing your current operation should be relatively easy; however it can be a lot harder task to decide what you plan to become.

So start by taking a step backward... and think outside the box. Then, answer a few questions:

- Who exactly are your customers?
- What products and services will you provide?
- And, what will you need to have in order to provide these items or services?
- When, in the form of a timeline will you provide these products or services?
- Where, demographically speaking are your customers?
- Why is there market or need for your business and is there a story to tell?
- How you will provide those products or services to your customer?

TIP
#2

The Business Name and the Executive Summary

The Executive Summary is a brief outline of the company purpose and goals. While it can be tough to fit on one or two pages, a good Summary includes:

- A brief description of products and service
- A summary of objectives
- A solid description of the market
- A high-level justification for viability (including a look atyour competition and your competitive advantage)
- A snapshot of growth potential
- An overview of funding requirements

The Executive Summary is often the make-or-break section of your business plan. A great business solves customer problems and shows how you'll make a profit. The summary shows how you plan to take advantage of a genuine opportunity. The "snapshot" of your business plan. Don't try to "hype" your business. Instead focus on what you plan to do, how you plan do it, and how you will succeed. Since a business plan should above all, help you start and grow your business.

The Executive Summary will first and foremost help you do the following.

1. Refine and tighten your concept. Think of it as a written "elevator pitch" (w/ more detail, of course). Your Summary

describes the highlights of your plan, includes only the most critical points, and leaves out less important issues and factors.

2. Determine your priorities. Your business plan walks the reader through your plan. What ranks high in terms of importance? Product development? Research? Innovation? Acquiring the right location? Creating strategic partnerships?

Your Summary serves as a guide to writing the rest of your plan.

In Review, include a:
• Brief description of products and services.
• A summary of objectives.
• A solid description of the market.
• A high-level justification for viability. (including a look at your competition and your competitive advantage)
• A snapshot of growth potential.
• An overview of funding requirements.

Your Mission Statement, Goals and Objectives

The best example of a mission statement will define a company and its purpose in 30 seconds or less. This is an expressive, concise paragraph that should be full of real meaning and impact.

Choose your words wisely – beware of buzzwords, empty phrases, or mission statements that are so general they could apply to many different companies. It's a challenge, but you want to capture what your company stands for in a brief and memorable way. A Mission Statement should answer questions people have about your business, like:

Who you are (your company)?
What do you do?
What do you stand for?
And why do you do what you do?
How you'll make a profit?
What markets are you serving, and benefits offered?
The problem you solve for customers?
Internal work environment do you want for your employees?

Unfortunately few mission statements are actually this good... that in mind,

> *Research well known Companies and how their mission statement defines them.*

Developing a useful mission statement in five easy steps:
1. Start with your market-defining story.
2. Define how your customer's life is better because your business exists.
3. Consider what your business does for employees.
4. Add what the business does for its owners.
5 Discuss, review, get honest opinions, and revise if needed.

In Review:
- The Company and its purpose in 30 seconds or less.
- A paragraph filled with meaning and impact.
- Be specific to your industry.
- What your company stands for.
- Be memorable...

Tips on Legal Structure, Permits/Licenses, and Insurance

In a nutshell, these are the business entities available to you. There are advantages and disadvantages for each. It's best to research legal structure in greater detail, or consult with an attorney and tax advisor if you're unsure as to the direction to take.

Sole Proprietorship - A sole proprietorship is the most basic type of business to establish. You alone own the company and are responsible for its assets and liabilities.

Liability Company - An LLC is designed to provide the limited liability features of a corporation and the tax efficiencies and operational flexibility of a partnership.

Cooperative - People form cooperatives to meet a collective need or to provide a service that benefits all member-owners.

Corporation - A corporation is more complex and generally suggested for larger, established companies with multiple employees.

Partnership - There are several different types of partnerships, which depend on the nature of the arrangement and partner responsibility for the business.

S Corporation - An S Corporation is similar to a C corporation but you are taxed only on the personal level.

In Review:
- Choose the legal structure that is right for your business.
- Research permit and licensing requirements for your type of business and location.
- Discuss insurance with a provider the coverage best suited for the product and/or services you offer.

Tips on Operations, Facility/Location, Equipment, Management/Personnel

This tip section details how to list the investment needed to start or expand the business and the expected financial performance of the business for the next three years based on this information.

The first of those documents is a list of what resources (examples; building, machinery, equipment, etc.) will be needed to open or expand the business. It should also explain how the costs of these resources will be financed either by the owner or an outside source of financing. Details supporting these costs should be included in an appendix to the business plan.

Management Summary (*example of the summary*)
The two managers, Ace Contractors, Inc. owner (listed here) and General Operations Manager (name), have impeccable credentials previously in our industry (Profile history of each).

This will benefit our company in three ways:
1. Clients will be brought from existing professional relationships
2. Respect and recognition by associated organizations and state departments.
3. The experience each has will attract new clients in the area of finance and administration.

(*Example continued*) - A Training Manager will be finalized in the coming year and will also include a Sales Manager and Contractor from within the industry. Their extensive experience and education in service, and management will provide a foundation for success.

Source of Funds and Use		
Source of Funds		
Owners and/or Other Investors	$	180,000
Bank Financing	$	200,000
Other Loans	$	50,000
Total Source of Funds	$	430,000
Use of Funding		
RealEstate/Buildings, Land, Etc	$	100,000
Leasehold Improvements	$	80,000
Capital for Equipment	$	80,000
Start-Up Inventory	$	25,000
Location and Admin Costs	$	18,000
Advertising & Promotional Costs	$	5,000
Other Expenses	$	2,000
Working Capital	$	100,000
Contingency Funds	$	20,000
Total Use of Funds	$	430,000

Personnel Plan (*example*)

By the end of June 2017, with the assumption of increased business volume, it will require that a Supervisor be added to our staff. By the end of August 2018, increased volume will require hiring additional staff in Operations.

In this example: Salaries of sales consultants, personnel, etc is included in the Cost of Sales. Only those costs for the hourly professional and administrative staff are shown in the Personnel table below.

	Year 1	Year 2	Year 3
Sales Consultants	$0	$10,000	$16,000
Operations Staff	$0	$40,000	$40,000
Trainers	$0	$0	$0
Additional Contractor(s)	$16,000	$32,000	$48,000
Admin Support	$10,000	$18,000	$28,000
Total Personnel	2	6	8
Total Payroll	$26,000	$100,000	$132,000

In Review:
- Detail the investment needed to start or expand the business.
- List of what resources (building, machinery, equipment, etc.)
- Explain how the costs of these resources will be financed.
- Create a management and personnel summary.

Building a Marketing Plan: Product/Service Description, Market Research, Target, and Competitive Analysis

Product/Service Description
This section of your business plan should give complete details on your product or services - and any variation to your industry to give the reader a clear understanding of what your company has to offer.

Your Market and Competitive Analysis
This section of your business plan should illustrate your industry and market knowledge as well as any of your research findings and conclusions. This section is usually presented after the company description.

What to Include in Your Market Analysis
Industry Description and Outlook – Describe your industry, including its current size and historic growth rate as well as other trends and characteristics. Next, list the major customer groups within your industry.

Information About Your Target Market – Narrow your target market to a manageable size. Many businesses make the mistake of trying to appeal to too many target markets.

Research and include the following information:
Distinguishing characteristics – What are the critical needs of your potential customers? Are those needs being met? What are the demographics of the group and where are they located? Are there any seasonal or cyclical purchasing trends that may impact your business?

Size of the primary target market – In addition to the size of your market, what data can you include about the annual purchases your market makes in your industry? What is the forecasted market growth for this group? For more information, search online for market research for tips and free government resources that can help you build a market profile.

In Review:
- Give complete details on your product or services
- Illustrate your industry, outlook, and market knowledge
- Supply information about your target market and size
- List distinguishing characteristics and critical needs

Tips on a Marketing Plan Budget: Pricing, Industry Trends, Marketing Costs

Marketing Plan/Budget Draft
This section of your business plan should give complete details on your marketing strategy - and any variation to your industry; to give the reader a clear understanding of how you'll get exposure in the marketplace.

More on Target Market and Competitive Analysis
Illustrate your industry and market knowledge as well as any of your research findings and conclusions.

What to Include in Your Marketing Plan
Marketing Timeline – Describe (list) your activities plan and how you'll take advantage of major opportunities to communicate with the customer.

Remember you are marketing to a manageable size. Many businesses make the same mistake of at first trying to market in too many areas. The timeline consists of activities that are free to utilize and some that cost on an ongoing basis. You can spend a million dollars on marketing with little success unless you're prepared to track results. Even then results can shift over time so be prepared to revise your marketing plan when needed.

Research data can also help in your decisions as to forecasted market growth for your industry. For more information, there are several free government resources that can help you build a marketing strategy including the US Census Bureau, the SBA Department, the Small

Business Development, and Economic Development Centers in your area.

In Review:
- Illustrate your industry, market knowledge, and research findings and conclusions.
- Marketing Timeline – Describe (list) your activities plan and how you'll take advantage of major opportunities.
- Cover Your Target Market – Marketing to a manageable size.

Creating a Financial Plan: Projected Revenue and Expense Statement, Cash Flow Projections, Break-even Analysis

Financial Statements

This section of your business plan support the three basic financial statements (1) **balance sheet**, which shows firm's assets, liabilities, and net worth on a stated date; (2) **income statement** (profit & loss account), and (3) **cash flow statement**, which shows the inflows and outflows of cash caused by activities during a stated period.

Break-even Point
Illustrate your total expenses; where your costs may be at any given point. And where sales volume should be at your break-even point based on

market research assumptions and conclusions. See break-even analysis chart.

Break-even Analysis

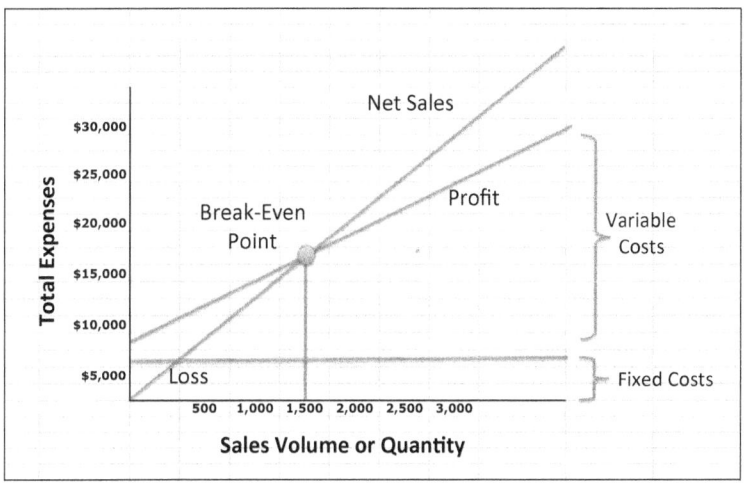

Balance Sheet: When researching various balance sheet templates, here are a couple of definitions to clarify:

Defining "Capital Stock"
Capital is defined as the total dollars a company receives to operate the business. Capital can be obtained by issuing stock (equity) or debt securities.

Companies with consistent corporate profits raise more firm capital by issuing debt, because the firm can generate income to make interest payments.

What are "Retained Earnings?"
Retained earnings refer to the percentage of net earnings not paid out as dividends, but retained by the company to be reinvested in its core business, or to pay debt.

25

In Review:
- Draft your three basic financial statements (1) balance sheet, (2) income statement, and (3) cash flow statement, based on research findings and conclusions.
- Illustrate or draft statement as to where your costs may be at any given point, and where sales volume should be at break-even point.
- More on all of this in Tip #9.

The Road to Financing: Summary of Financial Needs, Historical Financial Records, and Business/Personal Credit Report

1. Financial Statements Are Scorecards

Investors seek out quality companies with strong balance sheets, solid earnings and positive cash flow. Whether you're a do-it-yourself or rely on guidance from a professional, learning certain fundamental financial statement analysis skills can be very useful. Overly complex statistical analysis and formulas that don't convey information are not any better than straight talk about your business.

2. What Financial Statements to Use

For analysis purposes, the financial statements used are the balance sheet, the income statement, the cash flow statement as well as shareholders'/owners equity and retained earnings.

3. Knowing What's Behind the Numbers

The numbers in a company's financials reflect real world events. These numbers and the financial ratios/indicators for analysis are easier to understand if you can visualize the underlying realities of this essentially quantitative information.

One Time Start Up Expenses		Amount	Notes
Advertising and promotion			
Buildout/Renovations			
Cash for Operations			
Consulting Fees			
Decorating Painting and Remodeling			
Deposits and Public Utilities			
Equipment			
Furniture and Fixtures			
Legal and Professional Fees			
License and Permits			
One Time Start Up Costs			
Rent Deposit			
Software			
Starting Inventory			
Misc:			
Other:			
Total One Time Start Up Costs			

4. The Diversity of Financial Reporting

Don't expect financial statements to fit into a single mold. Simply remember that the diverse nature of your business activities results in a diversity of financial statement presentations.

5. The Challenge of Understanding Financial Jargon

The lack of any appreciable standardization of financial reporting terminology complicates the understanding of many financial statement account entries. This circumstance can be confusing for an investor, financial institution, etc.

6. Accounting Is an Art, Not a Science

The presentation of a company's financial position, as portrayed in its financial statements, is influenced by management estimates and judgments. In the best of circumstances, management should be conscientiously honest and candid.

Monthly Expenses		Amount	Notes
Bank Charges			
Debt Service (Principal and Interest)			
Insurance			
Maintenance and Repairs			
Marketing and Promotion: Ad			
Marketing and Promotion: Other			
Membership and Dues			
Misc:			
Payroll Tax			
Payroll: Wages (Employees)			
Payroll: Wages (Owner/Manager)			
Professional Fees: Accounting			
Professional Fees: Other			
Rent			
Subscriptions			
Supplies			
Telephone			
Utilities			
Other			
Total Mothly Expenses			
Number of months estimated to cover Expenses			

7. Non-Financial Statement Information

Information on the state of the economy, industry and competitive considerations, market forces, technological change, and the quality of management and the workforce are not directly reflected in a company's financial statements. Investors need to recognize that financial statement insights are but one piece, although an important one, of the larger investment information puzzle.

8. Financial Ratios and Indicators

The absolute numbers in financial statements are of little value for investment analysis, which must transform these numbers into meaningful relationships to judge a company's financial performance and condition. Beware of the one-size-fits-all syndrome that evaluative financial metrics can differ significantly by industry, company size and stage of development.

In Review:
- Draft a presentation that covers the 8 things you need to know about financial statements
- Create a start-up cost spreadsheet (utilizing template).
- Illustrate or draft assumptions as to where your sales/costs and cash flow may be with a financial projections spreadsheet (utilizing template).
- If financing is required, inquire into your business/personal credit history.

Check out these links for spreadsheets to use:
> Start-up Cost Spreadsheet: goo.gl/MUEJIZ
> Financial Projections Spreadsheet: goo.gl/la8nto

Drafting your Plan, Setting a Timetable, Key Contacts, Resumes, Marketing Materials, etc.

Following a timetable in essential in allowing the reader of you plan to understand what your business is all about. Displaying confidence in planning your strategy is important, not only for your investors or lenders but also your landlord when negotiating a lease agreement and ultimately your loyal "soon to be" customers.

Drafting your plan: The key components of your Business Plan.

Follow these 10 specific steps below when drafting your business plan. Spend the time reviewing and editing what you've come up with to ensure you have clearly made your points. The business model and concept you assemble is essentially your "dog and pony show," so with that in mind, you'll want to make a great first impression.

1. Business Name, Executive Summary
2. Mission Statement, Goals and Objectives
3. Legal Structure, Permits/Licenses, Insurance
4. Operations, Facility/Location, Equipment, Management/Personnel
5. Product/Service Description, Market Research, Target Analysis, Competitive Analysis
6. Marketing Plan: Pricing, Industry Trends, Marketing Plan and Marketing Budget
7. Financial Plan: Projected Revenue and Expense Statement, Cash Flow Projections, Break-even Analysis
8. Financial Plan: Summary of financial needs, Historical Financial Records, Business/Personal Credit Report Summary
9. Appendix: Timetable, Key Contacts, Resumes
10. Samples of Marketing Materials or Concepts, Lease/Rental Agreements, Contracts

Various Sources: Economic Trends and Research Data, Conference Board of Canada, and United States, U.S. Bureau of Labor and Statistics, Learning & Development Outlook Report, International Workplace Education, Wikipedia, the free encyclopedia, Training Studies and Tested Field Experience.

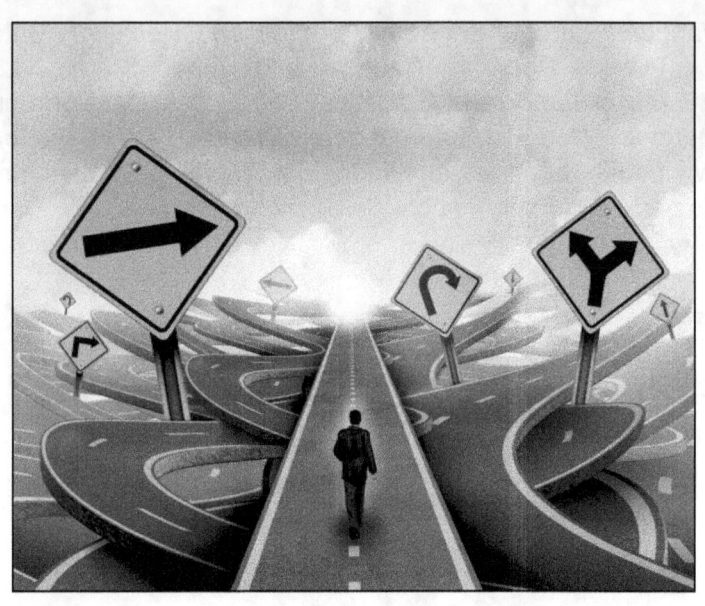

So There You Have It!
Guiding you on the best road to a business plan!

10 Ridiculously Simple Tips: Business Plans

Business Plan Tips in Review

1. Draft a Business Summary of Ideas and Overviews
2. The Business Name and the Executive Summary
3. Your Mission Statement, Goals and Objectives
4. Tips on Legal Structure, Permits/Licenses, and Insurance
5. Tips on Operations, Facility/Location, Equipment, Management/Personnel
6. Building a Marketing Plan: Product/Service Description, Market Research, Target, and Competitive Analysis

7. Tips on a Marketing Plan Budget: Pricing, Industry Trends, Marketing Costs
8. Creating a Financial Plan: Projected Revenue and Expense Statement, Cash Flow Projections, Break-even Analysis
9. The Road to Financing: Summary of Financial Needs, Historical Financial Records, and Business/Personal Credit Report
10. Drafting your Plan, Setting a Timetable, Key Contacts, Resumes, Marketing Materials, etc.

About the Author

John DeGaetano – *on the business side, John is a certified business advisor and works with businesses in guiding them in creating economic impact in the form of sales, jobs and market analysis. On the artistic side, John is the artistic director of a theatre company non-profit organization and author of several full length and 10-minute plays. His stage director credits include; Cats, Pirates of Penzance, Joseph and the Amazing Technicolor Dreamcoat, Chicago, West Side Story, and Evita to name a few. He's assisted with numerous other productions such as Miss Saigon along with Radio and Television work. His plays, informational books and presentations are available on Amazon, bookstores, and elsewhere.*

John DeGaetano Productions

More titles in the
10 Ridiculously Simple Tips Series

Includes:

Audition for the Stage
Business Plans
Financial Projections
Marketing
Motivation
Resume Writing
Sales
Social Networking
Stage Production
Training

www.ingramcontent.com/pod-product-compliance
Lightning Source LLC
Chambersburg PA
CBHW070724180526
45167CB00004B/1609